Lesson III
WRAPPING WITH A TWIST

Lesson IV
CREATIVE WRAPPING

52, Cornmarket Street, Oxford, OX1 3HJ England
AUSTRALIA AND NEW ZEALAND: Bookwise International, 174 Cornmack Road, Wingfield, SA 5013 Australia
ASIA & JAPAN: Japan Publications Trading Co., Ltd., 1-2-1, Sarugaku-cho, Chiyoda-ku, Tokyo, 101-0064 Japan

First printing: February 2004
Original Copyright © 2004 by Yoshiko Hase
World rights reserved. Published by JOIE, INC. 1-8-3, Hirakawa-cho, Chiyoda-ku, Tokyo 102-0093 Japan
Printed in Japan

ISBN 4-88996-129-1

LESSON I

WRAPPING BOXES NEATLY

Pretty wrapping begins with a simple gift box. Be reasonably generous with the paper, cut it to the right size, and make tight folds at the corners of the box. Be sure to use the best style for your gift, as it varies between the box shapes.

1

2

4

5

3

6

7

1 - 5   For instructions, see page 68
6 - 7   For instructions, see page 69

5

REGULAR WRAPPING (RECTANGULAR)

MATERIALS:
Paper: Embossed metallic Paper
Ribbon: Metallic sasheen
BOW: Star Bow (page 65)
TIE: Single Tie

SIZE OF PAPER

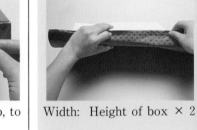

Length: Circumference of box plus 1" overlap

Width: Height of box × 2

5. Fold up the lower flap, to check the height.

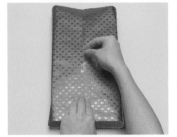

1. Center the box upside down on paper.

3. Work the ends. Tuck in shorter sides along the side edges of the box.

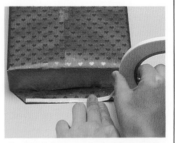

6. Unfold, and fold in the edge so that it just reaches the middle of box. Attach double-sided tape.

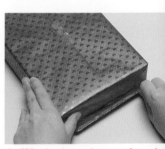

8. Work the other end as in Steps 3-7.

2. Overlap the side paper at the center, and tape to secure.

4. Fold down upper flap.

7. Fold back and secure.

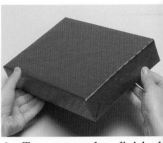

9. Turn over for finished parcel.

DIAGONAL WRAPPING

SIZE OF PAPER

Length: Use square-cut paper, and check that there is enough paper to cover the box with 3/4" extra at the corners.

Width: Check the remaining sides in the same manner.

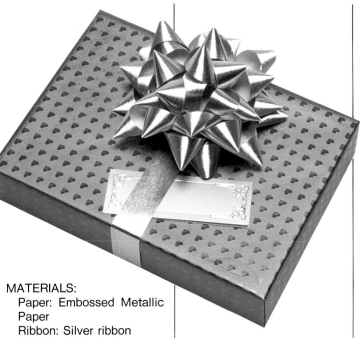

MATERIALS:
  Paper: Embossed Metallic Paper
  Ribbon: Silver ribbon
BOW: Star Bow (page 65)
TIE: Single Tie

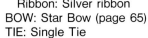

1. Center the box upside down, diagonally.

3. Tuck in the corner along the vertical edge of box.

2. Fold up the near end, pulling the paper tightly.

4. Fold up the rest so its folded edge aligns with the vertical edge of the box.

5. Fold over the box. (Beginners should tape the edge at this stage.)

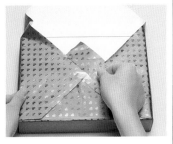

6. Fold the other side in the same manner, pulling the paper tightly.

7. Tuck in the far corners as in Step 3.

8. Fold over the remaining paper.

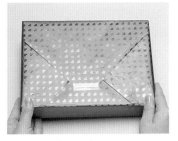

9. Tape the end.

10. Turn over for finished parcel.

7

ROLLED WRAPPING (RECTANGULAR)

SIZE OF PAPER

A: Position box 3/4" inside of the left-hand edge of paper.

B: Turn over the box and check that both of the far corners stay 3/4" inside of the paper.

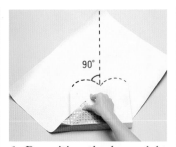

1. Reposition the box, right side up, so the left corner is 3/4" inside. Fold up the near end.

2. Tuck in the left side, pressing along the side edge of the box.

3. Lift the side paper so the folded edge aligns with the vertical edge of the box.

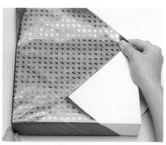

4. Make sharp folded edges, putting the paper tightly.

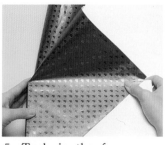

5. Tuck in the far corner along the side edge of the box.

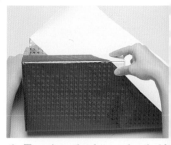

6. Turning the box, check if the folded edge aligns with the edge of the box.

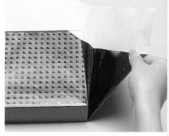

7. Turn the box over, and repeat Step 3.

8. Tape the far end as shown.

9. Lift remaining paper, folding to align the box.

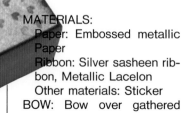

MATERIALS:
Paper: Embossed metallic Paper
Ribbon: Silver sasheen ribbon, Metallic Lacelon
Other materials: Sticker
BOW: Bow over gathered Lacelon (page 60)
TIE: Cross Tie (page 66)

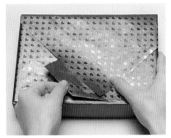

10. Bring the paper over.

11. Fold under any excess to align the edges.

12. Tape the end.

13. Turn over for finished parcel.

MATERIALS:
Paper: Embossed metallic Paper
Ribbon: Gold sasheen ribbon
Other materials: Sticker
BOW: Bow over gathered Lacelon
TIE: Cross Tie

1. Reposition the box, right side up, so the longer edge of box faces you. Fold up the near end.

2. Bring up the left side tightly to make a sharp edge.

SIZE OF PAPER

A: Position box 3/4" inside of the left-hand edge of paper.

B: Turn over the box and check that both of the far corners stay 3/4" inside of the paper.

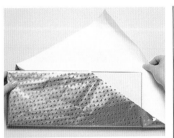

3. Turn the box over, adjusting the fold so it aligns with the edge of the box.

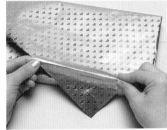

6. Fold the remaining paper aligning with the edge of the box. Fold under any excess.

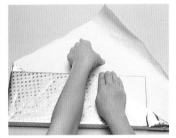

4. Pull the box toward you to take up the slack.

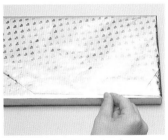

7. Tape the folded edge.

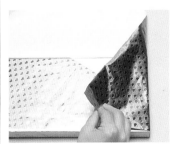

5. Fold the right side in the same manner as the other side.

8. Turn over for finished parcel.

9

REGULAR WRAPPING (SQUARE)

MATERIALS:
  Paper: Embossed metallic Paper
  Ribbon: Matching Satin ribbon, Narrow metallic ribbon
  Other materials: Wire
BOW: Fourfold Figure-8 Bow plus Double Figure-8 Bow
TIE: Double Cross Tie

SIZE OF PAPER

Length: Circumference of box plus 1" overlap

Width: Length of box plus two thirds height on each end.

1. Center the box wrong side up. Wrap around the box and tape. Tuck in shorter ends along the height of box.

2. Fold down upper flap. Fold lower flap so it ends exactly in the middle. Put double-sided tape along the edge.

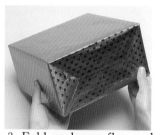

3. Fold up lower flap and press onto the tape

ROLLED WRAPPING (SQUARE)

MATERIALS:
  Paper: Embossed metallic Paper
  Ribbon: Matching Satin ribbon, Narrow metallic ribbon
  Other materials: Wire
BOW: Fourfold Figure-8 Bow plus Double Figure-8 Bow
TIE: Double Cross Tie

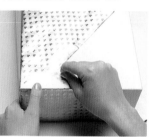

1. Place the box wrong side up so the left corner is 3/4" inside the paper. Fold up the near end and tuck in the left side along the height of box.

3. To cover the far right corner, fold up the right side.

2. Tucking in the excess paper to align with the edge of the box, turn the box.

4. Turn the box over, so the edge of the box aligns with the fold.

1. Center the box diagonally, wrong side up. Fold up the near end, then bring the left side up.

2. Fold the right side in the same manner and tape.

3. Tuck in remaining paper along the height of the box.

4. Bring over the paper and tape down.

MATERIALS:
  Paper: Embossed metallic Paper
  Ribbon: Matching Satin ribbon, Narrow metallic ribbon
  Other materials: Wire
BOW: Fourfold Figure-8 Bow plus Double Figure-8 Bow
TIE: Double Cross Tie

SIZE OF PAPER

When wrapped around, every corner should be entirely covered with 3/4" extra.

SIZE OF PAPER

Check as for page 8.

5. Bring over remaining paper and tape down.

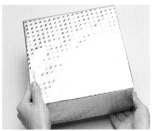

6. Turn over for finished parcel.

DIAGONAL WRAPPING (SQUARE)

WRAPPING POLYGON

MATERIALS:
Paper: Embossed metallic Paper

Ribbons: Metallic woven gold stripe ribbon, Narrow gold ribbon
Other materials: Wire 2 Stickers
BOW: Majo-Majo Bow
TIE: Arranged Cross Tie

1. Place the box on one side. Make a 3/8" fold on one side.

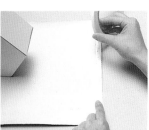

2. Stick double-sided tape on the fold for the same length as the height of the box.

3. Wrap around the box, so the papers overlap at an edge; tape down.

4. Make tucks toward the center point.

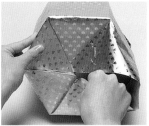

5. Be sure all the tucks are in the same direction.

SIZE OF PAPER

Width: Height of box plus half width of box.

Length: Circumference of box plus 1" overlap.

6. Secure the center with a sticker.

7. Place the box finished side down, and work as for Steps 4-5.

8. Insert the last tuck under the first tuck.

9. Attach a sticker for completed parcel.

MATERIALS:
  Paper: Patterned black paper
  Ribbon: Gold mesh ribbon, Narrow silver ribbon
  Other materials: Wire 2 Stickers, wire
BOW: Majo-Majo Bow
TIE: Single Tie

3. Fold down the right side along the edge, then fold the corner to make a neat apex.

7. Fold the flap and secure with a sticker.

1. Place the box as shown, fold on side of paper so their peaks meet.

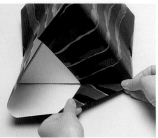

4. Fold again to align with the edge of the box.

8. Work the other side as for Steps 3-6.

2. Tuck in a side paper along the edge to make a neat corner.

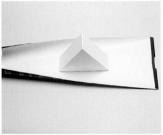

1. Center the box on one side. Make 3/8" fold on one end of paper.

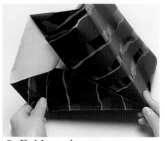

5. Fold up the paper.

9. Secure with a sticker.

3. Fold up the next side, tucking in any excess to adjust to the box.

2. Wrap around and tape at the apex edge.

6. Fold in the corners to make a triangular flap pointing to the center.

SIZE OF PAPER

Width: Height of box plus half width of box.

Length: Circumference of box plus 1"

EQUILATERAL TRIANGLE: B

MATERIALS:
  Paper: Patterned black paper
  Ribbon: Silver mesh ribbon
  Other materials: Sticker
BOW: Regular Bow Arranged Cross

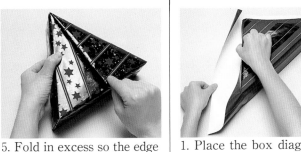

4. Fold up far side tucking in excess.

SIZE OF PAPER

When centered diagonally, the box must be entirely covered with 3/4"-1" overlap.

5. Fold in excess so the edge makes vertical center line.

1. Place the box diagonally, wrong side up. Fold up one corner so as to cover the wrong side, with 3/4" extra.

6. Secure with a sticker for completed parcel.

2. Tuck in paper along the edge of box to make a neat corner.

WRAPPING ISOSCELES TRIANGLE

3. Tuck in excess to align with the edge of box; secure with double-sided tape.

SIZE OF PAPER

Square paper to entirely cover the box and overlap on sides. (Fold in half to adjust the size)

4. Work the other side in the same manner.

6. Tuck in excess to align with the box; secure with double-sided tape.

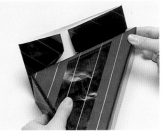

5. Fold up the remaining side, tucking in along side edges of the box.

MATERIALS:
  Paper: Striped black paper
  Ribbon: Silver mesh ribbon, Narrow silver ribbon
  Other materials: Sticker, Wire
BOW: Majo-Majo Bow (page 63)
Tie: Single Tie

WRAPPING HAT BOX

Width: Diameter plus height of box minus 3/8"

Length: Circumference of box plus 1" overlap.

7. Work the other side in the same manner.

8. Attach sticker to the center.

MATERIALS:
   Paper: Glossy paper with colorful pattern
   Ribbon: Metallic curling ribbons
   Other materials: Stickers, Wire
BOW: Majo-Majo Bow (page 63)
Tie: Arranged Cross Tie

1. Place the box as shown, in the center of paper width. Fold 3/8" on one side.

4. Make tucks toward the center point. Make sure the tucks face the same direction.

2. Attach double-sided tape in the same length as the height of box.

5. Insert the last tuck under the first. When finished, there is a 3/8" hole in the center.

3. Wrap around and press down the tape.

6. Attach a sticker to the center.

WRAPPING CYLINDRICAL BOX

1. Cover 2/3 of the circumference of box.

2. Fold one side.

3. Make tucks so as to end with one point.

4. After making 4 to 5 tucks, make sure the last fold is perpendicular to the working table.

5. Work the other side in the same manner.

7. Roll the box, tucking in any excess paper.

6. Tuck in excess paper so as to align with the edge of box.

8. Secure with a sticker.

MATERIALS:
  Paper: Glossy paper with colorful pattern
  Ribbon: Metallic curling ribbons
  Other materials: Sticker
BOW: Single Bow (page 60)
Tie: Cross Tie (page 66)

SIZE OF PAPER

Square paper, each side measuring height and diameters of box plus 3/4"-1".

USING THE SHAPE OF THE GIFT

9

8

11

13

12

Gift that do not fit into boxes
can be wrapped up in a pretty way
making the most of the natural shapes.
Make pleats, gathers or whatever nice,
and enjoy your wrapping!

15

14

8 - 11   For instructions, see page 69.
12 - 15   For instructions, see page 70.

1. Place the bottle diagonally on paper so the bottom is entirely covered with 1" extra.

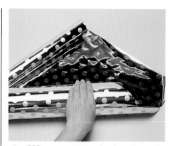

2. Wrap around the bottle, starting with near corner.

3. When 2/3 of the circumference is covered, lift right side paper.

4. Make tucks so as to end at one point.

MATERIALS:
  Paper: Metallic cellophane with dots
  Ribbon: Satin ribbon with dots, Narrow gold ribbon
  Other materials: Sticker, Wire
BOW: Majo-Majo Bow (page 63)
Tie: Bind bottle neck.

5. After making 4-5 tucks, make sure the last fold is perpendicular to the working surface.

6. Roll the bottle, tucking in any excess paper.

7. Secure the corner edge with a sticker.

8. Gather at the bottle neck.

1. Stand the bottle in the center of paper.

2. Make tucks toward the neck all around.

3. Check if all pleats are even.

4. Hold the bottle by the neck and the bottom, twist in opposite directions as you would wring a towel.

WRAPPING PLUMP BOTTLE

CANDY WRAPPING

1. Use 2 sheets of paper of different colors. Attach double-sided tape along the edge of one sheet and join.

MATERIALS:
Paper: Metallic cellophane with dots, Black matt-finish cellophane with dots
Ribbon: Satin ribbon with dots, in black and white
Other materials: Sticker, Wire
BOW: Single Bow (page 60)

MATERIALS:
Paper: Black mat-finish cellophane with dots
Ribbon: Satin ribbon with dots, Narrow gold ribbon
Other materials: Sticker, Wire
BOW: Majo-Majo Bow (page 63)
Tie: Bind bottle neck.

2. Center sweater bound with ribbon on the joined paper.

4. Gather both ends and secure with wire.

3. Wrap around and secure with a sticker.

5. Finished parcel.

5. Finished parcel.

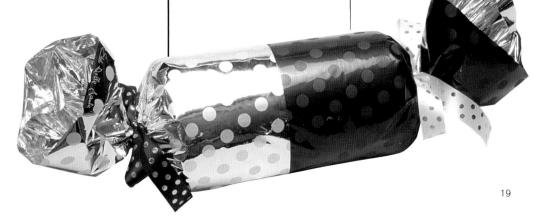

WRAPPING POT PLANT

WRAPPING FLOWERED BASKET

MATERIALS:
Paper: Cellophane with check pattern, Wrinkled *washi* paper
Ribbons: Woven sheer ribbon
Other materials: Wire
BOW: Fivefold French Bow
TIE: Wind the pot with streamers.

2. Fold near end of cellophane inside, pull the pot toward you, and lift up layered paper just to cover the height of pot.

3. Pull the side up and backward, so as to fit the pot shape.

1. Lay Washi over cellophane, then center the pot.

4. Draw up all around, making pleats; staple to secure at several places.

1. Lay two sheets of paper as shown and center flower basket.

2. Fold over the paper just to cover the basket. Work the back in the same manner.

MATERIALS:
Paper: *Unryu-washi*, in dark and light shades
Ribbon: Metallic curling ribbons
TIE: Curl Reflex and lay across the flowers.

3. Draw up side and make pleats.

4. Staple both sides to secure the pleats.

WRAPPING BOUQUET

MATERIALS:
  Paper: Clear cellophane with floral pattern, Thick green paper
  Ribbon: Brown ribbon with pattern, Tube ribbon
TIE: Fivefold French Bow

1. Adjust the size of paper so the two sheets are the same size.

2. Put bouquet between two sheets. Fold near edges of the sheets together twice.

3. Secure the fold by stapling at 4 places.

4. Fold far ends of paper as well. Finally, fold the top edges twice and staple. Now three sides are sealed.

5. Gather paper on the stem side.

WRAPPING BALL

WRAPPING MELON

MATERIALS:
Paper: Mat brown paper with map pattern
Ribbons: Dark satin ribbon
Other materials: Wire
BOW: Fourfold French Bow (Stuck on top with double-sided tape)

1. Lay two sheets of paper and center melon.

3. Tuck in shorter folds to secure.

1. Cut out paper in the round that covers the ball.

4. Be sure to make even tucks in the same direction.

2. Join all corners.

4. Gather at the top.

MATERIALS:
Paper: *Unryu - washi* in white and mustard
Ribbon: Satin ribbons in frosty colors
Other materials: Wire
BOW: Majo-Majo Bow (Page 63)
TIE: Twist the top and tie a bow.

2. Center the ball.

5. Keep folding until there is no paper left.

5. Spread the paper out for a neat finish.

3. Lift up near side, and make tucks toward one point.

6. Tape down for finished parcel.

6. Finished parcel.

WRAPPING TEDDY

3. Fold paper in half at the center so the fold makes the bottom.

4. Check the shape of the teddy.

MATERIALS:
Paper: Clear cellophane with check pattern
Ribbons: Red ribbon with pattern
Other materials: Sticker
TIE: Bind the top and tie a bow.

1. Place the teddy, face down, so the feet are positioned at the center.

5. Gather the paper above the head of the teddy.

2. Wrap around loosely, overlapping sides entirely; secure with a sticker.

6. Spread the paper out, resembling flower petals.

WRAPPING UMBRELLA

1. Cut paper according to the length of umbrella. Take some extra width so the umbrella is loosely wrapped.

4. Put the umbrella through.

2. Attach double-sided tape along one longer edge of paper.

5. Gather the paper around the handle.

3. Press down to make a cylindrical shape.

6. Gather at the other side.

BOW: Pull the thread of Piccolo
Bow to make a bow shape. (Page 44)
TIE: Curl Reflex and tie Piccolo
Bow at both ends.

MATERIALS:
Paper: Metallic cellophane with floral pattern
Ribbon: Metalic curling ribbon
Other materials: Sticker

LESSON III
WRAPPING WITH A TWIST

For those who are not satisfied
with authentic wrapping,
or who want to express yourself,
here are some up-graded ideas.
A little accessory or arrangement
will go a long way.

16

20

16   For instructions, see page 70
17 - 22 For instructions, see page 71

18

19

21

22

PLEATED WRAPPING: A (Vertical Pleats)

1. Make a wide fold in the center, tucking its sides under.

3. Secure pleats from wrong side with tape. Place the box so the wide fold aligns with the center of box. Tape to secure.

5. Fold up lower flap; tape.

5. Fold up lower flap; tape.

2. Make folds on both sides of this fold.

4. To finish sides, fold down pleated flap first.

6. Finished parcel.

MATERIALS:
  Paper: Metallic paper
  Ribbon: Silvery tube-type ribbon
    BOW: Double Figure-8 Bow plus half bow (Attach with double-sided tape)

SIZE OF PAPER

Width: Height of box

Length: Circumference of box plus pleats

SIZE OF PAPER

A: Position box as for Diagonal Wrapping, and check the size by turning it over.

B: Adjust the size as for Diagonal Wrapping, by adding extra for pleats.

1. Fold the paper in half lengthwise.

2. Pre-fold the pleats by folding in the same direction.

PLEATED WRAPPING:
C (Asymmetrical Pleats)

MATERIALS:
Paper: Metallic paper
Ribbon: Brown tube-type ribbon
BOW: Triple Figure-8 Bow, secured by tying a knot (Attach with double-sided tape)

SIZE OF PAPER

Length: Circumference of box plus pleat portion.

3. Unfold. Using the creases, make pleats until there is paper enough for Diagonal Wrapping.

1. Fold about 3/8" on one side of paper.

4. Unfold. Using the creases, make pleats tucking under 3/8" each.

6. Fold down upper (pleated) flap, then fold up lower flap.

4. Place the box so the pleats cross diagonally. Wrap as for Diagonal Wrapping.

2. Fold again, wider than the previous fold.

5. On wrong side of paper, secure pleats with tape, at the same time checking if the paper edges meet on wrong side of box.

7. Finished parcel.

5. Finished parcel.

3. Fold again, even wider. (Make as many pleats as you like.)

MATERIALS:
Paper: Metallic paper
Ribbon: Gold tube-type ribbon
BOW: Sixfold Figure-8 Bow (Attach with double-sided tape.)

27

WRAPPING WITH EXTRA: A (Inserted Strips)

WRAPPING WITH EXTRA: B (Pointed Flap)

MATERIALS:
Paper: Glossy
paper, in black
and red
Ribbon: Red
satin ribbon
Other Mate-
rials: Sticker
BOW: Single
Bow
TIE: Single Tie

1. Be sure to have more overlap than in the Regular Wrapping. (Page 6)

4. Using the black paper, make a triangle.

1. Use paper that covers the box and overlap entirely, as shown.

4. Fan out strips and staple. (Make two.)

2. Make a 4" slit into the center on one edge of paper.

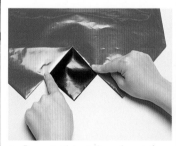

5. Insert this triangle under the flap and align the peaks: Secure with double-sided tape.

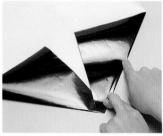

2. Fold up corners to make triangular end.

5. Put strips under the tri-angular flap and shape: mark attaching positions. Attach double-sided tape at marks; press down.

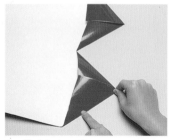

3. Fold in the corners to make two triangles.

6. Wrap the box. Bring over flap to a position you like. Attach double-sided tape onto the wrong side of paper and secure. Finish the sides as for Regular Wrapping.

3. Cut the extra paper into strips. Fold in half and seal with double-sided tape.

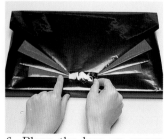

6. Place the box on paper and secure with a sticker. Finish the sides as for Regu-lar Wrapping.

MATERIALS:
Paper: Glossy
paper, in red
and black
Ribbon: Black
satin ribbon
Other Mate-
rials: Sticker
BOW: Single
Bow
TIE: Single Tie
with double
strand

WRAPPING WITH EXTRA: C (Inserting Paper Doileys)

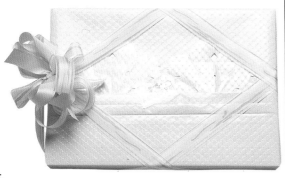

MATERIALS:
Paper: Glossy quilt paper, in pastels
Ribbon: Woven sheer ribbon, Satin
ribbon Other Materials: Sticker

BOW: Majo-Majo Bow
TIE: Double Diagonal Tie

1. Cut out a square for doiley.

4. Unfold and cut in half.

2. Fold twice to make a smaller square, then fold into thirds.

5. Prepare a finished parcel, wrapped by Regular Wrapping method with pleats.

3. Using pinking shears, trim the edges. Make incisions on folded sides.

6. Insert doiley halves under pleats.

WRAPPING WITH EXTRA: D (Reversible Effect)

1. Using double-sided tape, stick blue paper onto the wrong side of pink paper.

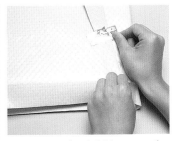

3. Secure the fold by attaching a sticker.

2. Fold over the edge so as to show the color of the wrong side. (Take appropriate width.)

4. Finish the sides as for Regular Wrapping. (Lower flap is folded over the upper flap.)

MATERIALS:
Paper: Glossy quilt paper
Ribbon: Woven sheer ribbon, Satin ribbon
Other Materials: Sticker
BOW: Majo-Majo Bow
TIE: Cross Tie

WRAPPING WITH JOINED PAPER: A

MATERIALS:
  Paper: Glossy paper, in solid and patterned
  Ribbon: Sheer ribbon with gold trim, Narrow satin ribbon
  Other Materials: Wire
  BOW: Sixfold Figure-8 Bow
  TIE: Cross Tie (Page 66)

3. Center the box and wrap around. Fold down overlap diagonally. (Make a slant to your liking.)

1. Fold up 3/4" of one paper, attach double-sided tape along the fold.

4. Secure with double-sided tape.

2. Join the other paper carefully to make a straight line

5. Finish the sides as for Regular Wrapping.

WRAPPING WITH JOINED PAPER: B

1. Center the box right side up. Fold back both ends of paper to the wrong side.

5. Finish the sides as for Regular Wrapping. (Size of the inner paper can be adjusted in Step 1.)

2. Cut out the other paper so it just covers the top side.

3. Attach double-sided tape along both ends of paper.

4. Lift up both sides and press down along the tape.

MATERIALS:
  Paper: Glossy paper, in solid and patterned
  Ribbon: Sheer ribbon with gold trim, Narrow satin ribbon
  Other Materials: Wire
  BOW: Sixfold Figure-8 Bow
  TIE: Cross Tie (Page 66)

WRAPPING WITH JOINED PAPER: C (Large Box: A)

1. Join two sheets of the black paper with double-sided tape to make a large sheet.

2. Make a pleated section with white paper, folding the center as for a box pleat.

MATERIALS:
Paper: Glossy paper, in black and white
Ribbon: Red satin ribbon
Other Materials: Wire
BOW: Fourfold Figure-8 Bow
TIE: Cross Tie (Page 66)

3. Place pleated section on top of box.

5. Attach double-sided tape and stick edges of black paper onto sides of the pleated section.

4. Fold up both side edges of joined paper.

6. Finish the sides as for Regular Wrapping. See Regular Wrapping for the size of paper.

WRAPPING WITH JOINED PAPER: B (Large Box: B)

1. Join two sheets of the same paper with double-sided tape to make a large sheet.

4. Place pleated sheet on top of the wrong side of box. Check the position and join with the larger sheet.

2. Fold up corners of one end to make a peaked edge.

5. As for Regular Wrapping, attach double-sided tape onto the wrong side of pleated sheet and press onto box.

3. Prepare pleated section with another paper. (Secure with tape across the wrong side.)

6. Finish the sides as for Regular Wrapping. See page 28 for the size of paper.

MATERIALS:
Paper: Glossy paper, in black and white
Color (Black and White)
Ribbon: Satin ribbon, in varied widths
Other Materials: Wire
BOW: Majo-Majo Bow
TIE: Cross Tie

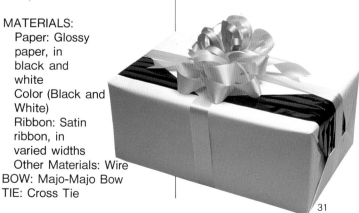

RECTANGULAR FOLD

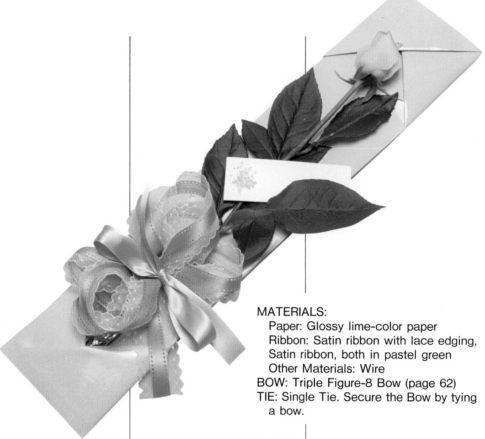

Width: Width of flower ×
3

Length: Length of flower
× 1.5

MATERIALS:
  Paper: Glossy lime-color paper
  Ribbon: Satin ribbon with lace edging,
  Satin ribbon, both in pastel green
  Other Materials: Wire
BOW: Triple Figure-8 Bow (page 62)
TIE: Single Tie. Secure the Bow by tying
  a bow.

1. Fold paper into thirds lengthwise.

3. Fold back diagonally, away from you.

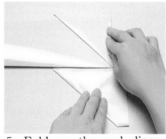

5. Fold up the end diagonally.

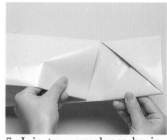

7. Join two envelopes by inserting plain end into the pocket, each other to make a stiff sheet.

2. Bring up one side to cover most of the flower stem.

4. Fold the end underneath.

6. Insert the peak under the triangle made in step 3. With another sheet of paper, make another envelope.

8. Insert flower.

TRIANGULAR FOLD

1. Fold paper in thirds to make a rectangle.

4. Fold again until there is no paper left.

6. Put the gift in.

2. Fold one end at an angle of 60°.

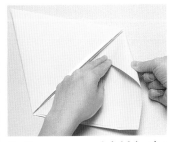

5. Turn over and fold in the excess.

7. Tuck in the remaining flap to close the envelope.

8. Finished parcel.

3. Bring this new fold to align with the long fold. Fold again in the same manner.

MATERIALS:
Paper: Glossy beige paper
Ribbon: Woven gold ribbons, in varied widths and patterns
BOW: Double Bow
TIE: Arrangement of Cross Tie

BIG MEDICINAL WRAP

This wrapping method needs no sticky tape as it secures itself. Attach a sticker, if preferred.

2. Fold diagonally in half.

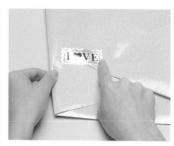

4. Secure the end with a sticker.

6. Fold down far left edge as shown.

1. Cut out a square paper.

3. Fold up both sides, dividing the folded edge into thirds, as shown.

5. Put gift in.

7. Fold down far right edge so it covers the folds.

MATERIALS:
  Paper: Glossy lime-color paper
  Ribbons: Woven satin ribbon in icy green
  Other Materials: Wire, Seal
BOW: Attach Double Bow with double-sided tape.

8. Tuck in excess under the first folds.

9. Finished Medicinal Wrap.

34

FOLDED BOX

MATERIALS:
  Paper: Glossy pale pink paper
  Ribbons: Soft nylon tulle ribbon in lime color
BOW: Triple Figure-8 Bow
TIE: Cross Tie (Page 66)

1. Cut paper, to about B4 size (14" × 10").

2. Fold up in half.

3. Fold in half the other way.

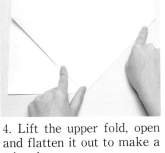

4. Lift the upper fold, open and flatten it out to make a triangle.

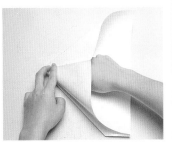

5. Turn over and fold as for back.

6. Bring over the left side flap. Turn over and repeat.

7. Fold in right side to meet the center. Fold in left side the same.

8. Turn over and fold as for back.

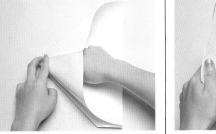

9. Open out and crease four sides to form a box.

10. Put gift in.

11. Pull up sides toward the center.

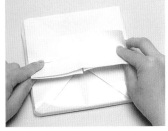

12. Fold back so the folded edges meet precisely.

13. Completed parcel.
* Notes: Adjust the size of paper according to the size of gift. For example, a CD needs B4 paper.

WRAPPING WITH FUROSHIKI

MATERIALS:
  Wrapper: Medium-sized
  Furoshiki
  Ribbon: Satin ribbon
BOW: Bind the neck of bottle
  and tie a bow.

3. Roll the bottle until there is no cloth left.

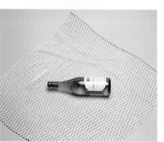

1. Lay bottle on the diagonal, a little lower than center.

4. Tie both ends over the rolled end.

2. Wrap the cloth around the bottle.

5. Tie a knot for completed parcel.

WRAPPING WITH NAPKIN

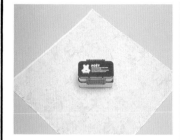

1. Center lunch box.

3. Bring over the far corner.

2. Bring near corner over the lunch box.

4. Lift up sides, making gathers.

WRAPPING WITH SCARF

MATERIALS:
  Wrappers: Medium sized scarf. Patterned tissue

5. Make a knot at the center.

5. Tie over the handle.

6. Finished look.

1. Fold scarf into the same width as basket.

3. Lift up sides and cross each other.

6. Tie into a bow.

MATERIALS:
  Wrapper: 20" square napkin
  Ribbon: Satin ribbon
BOW & TIE: Bow on Single Tie

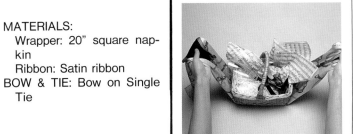

2. Center the basket.

4. Pass one side round the handle.

7. Finished look.

37

LESSON IV
CREATIVE WRAPPING

Hand-made gift in hand-made
package —— what else could
make you happier?
Unusual things may turn into
a greatest giftbox.
The following pages will
present such "wrapping ideas".

23

24

23 - 28 For instructions, see page 72
29 For instructions, see page 73

26

27

29

25

28

MAKING PAPER BAG (With Gusset)

1. Fold lengthwise in half, to mark the center line.

2. Unfold. Fold up near edge to meet the center.

4. Fold up the bottom part. (Make a large fold for thick bag, small fold for thin bag.)

8. Attach double-sided tape onto lower flap, all along edges.

3. Fold down far edge to overlap 1/5", join with double-sided tape.

5. Open the corners and flatten to make triangles.

9. Fold up and press. Make creases to form gussets.

MATERIALS:
Paper: Glossy paper with dots
Ribbon: Satin ribbons, in varied widths and shades
Other Materials: Sticker
BOW: Arranged Double Wave Bow (Attach with double-sided tape.)

6. Fold down the joined flap to meet the center.

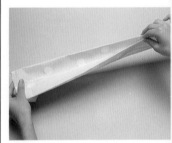

10. Pressing with your left thumb, make creases lengthwise.

7. Unfold and attach double-sided tape above the folded line. (Do not attach tape if the wrong side of paper peaks out.) Fold down and stick.

11. Completed bag. (Various sized bags can be made depending on the size of paper or gusset width.)

MAKING A SHIRT-COLLAR BAG

MAKING A FLAT BAG

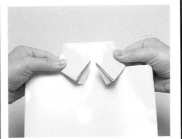

3. With the right side of bag up, fold both flaps to form a 'collar'.

MATERIALS:
   Paper: Glossy paper with dots
   Ribbon: Satin ribbon
Other Materials: Sticker
TIE: Wrap around the edge and tie a bow.

MATERIALS:
   Paper: Glossy paper with dots
   Ribbon: Satin ribbon in matching color
TIE: Wrap around neck and tie a bow.

4. Fold cut edges under at a slant to form 'shoulders'.

1. Fold both sides to overlap 1/5" at the center; secure with double-sided tape.

4. Cut off upper fold (joined side).

1. Make a bag with gusset.

5. Open 'shoulders' and fold excess inside along the 'shoulder' line.

2. Fold up the bottom edge.

5. Attach double-sided tape onto the wrong side, fold up and press.

2. Fold the open edge twice. Make slits just under the fold, to one third of the width from each side.

6. Completed bag.

3. Unfold and cut off corners.

6. Completed bag.

41

DECORATING BOX: A

1. Using a knife, make slits on the lid of commercial box, on both sides.

2. Pass ribbon through the slits, around the box.

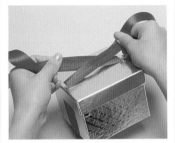

MATERIALS:
   Ribbon: Satin ribbon, Narrow metallic ribbon
   Other Materials: Wire, Scissors
   BOW: Majo-Majo Bow (page 63)

3. Pull ribbon so the lid is secured.

DECORATING BOX: B

1. Use ribbons in assorted colors and widths.

2. Pre-wrap the box and cut off excess.

DECORATING BOX: C

MATERIALS:
  Ribbons: Satin ribbons in varied colors
  Other Materials: Wire
BOW: Majo-Majo Bow (page 63)
TIE: Cross Tie

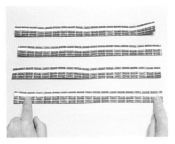

1. Attach double-sided tape along the wrong side of 4 strips of ribbon.

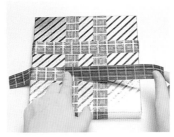
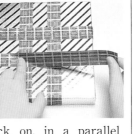

3. Stick on, in a parallel pattern.

5. Have Christmas ornaments ready.

3. Attach double-sided tape along each ribbon.

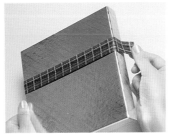

2. Stick ribbon onto the lid of box; fold ends inside the lid.

4. Prepare ribbon as in Step 1; stick onto the box to match with the lid.

6. Using a Glue Gun, attach ornaments.

4. Stick ribbons onto box in a balanced manner.

7. Checking the balance, attach all the remaining ornaments.

MATERIALS:
  Ribbon: Tartan plaid ribbon with gold stripes
  Other Materials: Christmas ornaments
BOW: Fourfold French Bow

5. Finished box.

43

MAKING PYRAMID PACKAGE

MATERIALS:
  Paper: Glossy paper with pattern
  Ribbon: Gold striped ribbon
  Other Materials: Flat paper bag
BOW: Single Bow

1. Use a commercial flat paper bag.

2. Open the bag and press sides so the folded lines meet.

4. Pass ribbon and fold in.

3. Fold the opening to form a triangle.

5. Fold again.

PICCOLO BOW
(page 23)

1. Cut to the length as appropriate (about 12").

2. Pull both ends of inner string. Attractive bow is made in an instant.

MAKING APPLE SHAPED PACKAGE

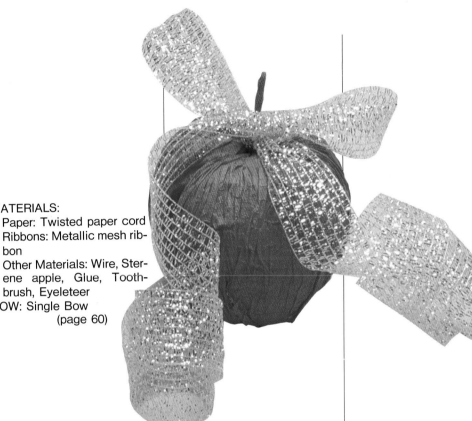

MATERIALS:
Paper: Twisted paper cord
Ribbons: Metallic mesh ribbon
Other Materials: Wire, Sterene apple, Glue, Toothbrush, Eyeleteer
BOW: Single Bow
(page 60)

7. Wrap with Penelope.

8. Wrap each half. Using eyeleteer, pierce one half to stick a stem. Wrap wire with Penelope and stick in.

1. Cut a styrene apple vertically in half.

3. Unwind Penelope.

5. Trim to fit the apple half. Make two.

9. Put the gift in.

2. Using a knife, make a cavity to put gift in.

4. Open out Penelope and flatten.

6. Using a tooth brush, apply glue all over the apple.

10. Join halves.

45

USING LADLE AS GIFTBOX

USING MUG AS GIFTBOX

MATERIALS:
Paper: Clear cellophane with floral pattern
Ribbon: Metallic curling ribbons, in varied widths and colors
BOW: Triple Figure-8 Bow

2. Put gift in (Shown above are candies).

1. Use a large mug.

3. Hold paper with the bottom of handle.

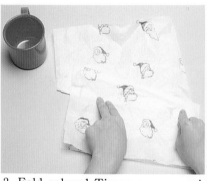

2. Fold colored Tissue as appropriate, to make uneven edges.

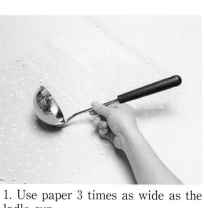

1. Use paper 3 times as wide as the ladle cup.

4. Gather paper, making neat pleats.

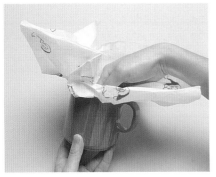

3. Lay the mug with Colored tissue.

4. Stuff with packing to give a height.

5. Put gift in.

MATERIALS:
  Paper: Clear cellophane with floral pattern, Patterned tissue
  Ribbon: Striped mesh ribbon
  Other materials: Packing
BOW & TIE: Bind at sides and tie a bow each.

DECORATING JAR

MATERIALS:
  Ribbon: Metallic ribbon in geometric pattern
  Other Materials: Wire, Jar
BOW: Double Bow (Attach with double-sided tape.)

1. Adjust the ribbon length to the height of jar. Cut off excess.

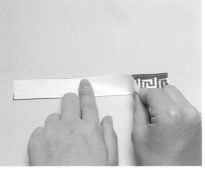

2. Attach double-sided tape along the wrong side of ribbon. (Use tape of the same width as the ribbon, for the wrong side of ribbon can be seen through glass.)

3. Stick ribbons.

4. Stick ribbons of various colors.

5. Stick ribbons all around the jar for finished gift.

WRAPPING COMMON SENSE

For Boys

For Girls

GIFT FOR BABIES

Express the delicateness of the baby by choosing soft hues like pastels.

MATERIALS:
  Paper: Pale solid-color paper
  Ribbon: Striped ribbon
  Other Materials: Wire
WRAP: Diagonal Wrapping (page 7)
BOW: Triple Figure-8 Bow
TIE: Diagonal Tie (page 66)

GIFT FOR CHILDREN

Children prefer distinctive patterns or vivid colors. Combinations of complementary colors are also their favorite.

MATERIALS:
  Paper: Glossy paper with animal pattern
  Ribbon: Striped satin ribbon in matching colors
WRAP: Diagonal Wrapping (page 7)
BOW & TIE: Cross Tie + Single Bow at center

GIFT FOR TEENAGERS

Considering their tendencies to copy adults, make a combination that expresses a grown-up image, yet with some purity.

MATERIALS:
  Paper: Glossy paper in tartan plaid
  Ribbon: White satin ribbon with dots
  Other Materials: Wire
WRAP: Equilateral Wrapping: A (page 12)
BOW & TIE: Arrangement of Cross Tie + Triple Figure-8 Bow

For Men

For Women

GIFT FOR YOUNGSTERS

Simple wrapping expresses youth. Choose similar shades and add simple bows.

MATERIALS:
Paper: White paper with simple pattern
Ribbon: Narrow satin ribbon
WRAP: Diagonal Wrapping
BOW & CROSS: Double Cross Tie + Single Bow

GIFT FOR ADULTS

Add gold colors for a festive look. Choose paper in quiet hues to enhance the ribbon.

MATERIALS:
Paper: Glossy paper in dark color
Ribbon: Golden striped ribbon
WRAP: Diagonal Wrapping
BOW & TIE: Cross Tie + Single Bow

MATERIALS:
Paper: Glossy paper with colorful pattern
Ribbon: Golden Striped ribbon
Other Materials: Wire
WRAP: Diagonal Wrapping (Page 7)
BOW & TIE: Diagonal Tie + Triple Figure-8 Bow

GIFT FOR SENIORS

Choose gentle colors and add a touch of vividness. Display a gorgeous image on the whole.

MATERIALS:
Paper: Glossy paper with intricate gold pattern
Ribbon: Satin ribbon in dark brown
Other Materials: Sticker
WRAP: Diagonal Wrapping
BOW & TIE: Cross Tie + Single Bow at center

MATERIALS:
Paper: Glossy paper with gentle-color pattern
Ribbon: Satin ribbon
Other Materials: Wire
WRAP: Hat Box Wrapping
BOW & TIE: Arrangement of Diagonal Tie + Triple Figure-8 Bow

FOR EACH HAPPY SCENE

Gifts for Women

**Create an elegant mood with wrapping
paper and ribbon.**

30 - 34 For instructions, see page 74

ifts for Men

Use blue or beige shades to give
a sound and intellectual image.

35 - 39 For instructions, see page 75

Bridal Showers

Fashion your giftbox with shiny white and gold ribbons, which conveys your very best wishes for the couple's new life.

40 - 45 For instructions, see page 76

40

41

44

42

43

45

Mother's Day

To the mother who always loves you so deeply and gently like the soothing shade of lavender.

46 - 50 For instructions, see page 77

Father's Day

To the reliable hero, kind and energetic. You'll always stay this way!

51 - 55 For instructions, see page 78

St. Valentine's Day

62 - 69 For instructions, see page 80

62

63

64

65

66

67

68

69

Holiday Gifts

Christmas is the happiest season of the year.
Presents wrapped in red and green
will bring excitement for everyone.

70 - 78 For instructions, see page 81.

SEASONAL WRAPPING

Recently it has become more difficult to express
season by season. Gift-dressing with a seasonal touch
will appear all the more impressive.

Spring

Summer

79 80

81 82

Autumn

Winter

79 - 82 For instructions, see page 73

BEFORE WRAPPING UP

1 Wire
2 Cellotape
3 Stapler
4 Double-sided tape
5 Eyeleteer
6 Toothbrush
7 Paper knife

8 Knife
9 Glue (for wood)
10 Glue Gun
11 Wire-cutting scissors
12 Scissors
13 Pinking shears

NOTES FOR SUCCESSFUL WRAPPING:

Be reasonably generous with the paper and cut to fit the box.
When deciding the size of paper, place the actual object on.
Carefully cut the paper so as to show the pattern in its best.
Use heavyweight, stiff paper for Regular Wrapping and Diagonal Wrapping.

When wrapping with gathers or decorative folds, use softer paper.

Fragile objects or things that cannot be turned over should be wrapped with right side up.
It is wise to use the wrapping method that shows the joint of paper on the right side.
Avoid diagonal ribbon tie when wrapping high boxes.

Use double-sided tape for neater wrapping.
Adjust the size of ribbon bow and width to the object.
Be flexible and create your own wrappers other than papers.
Accompany the gift with a greeting card or accessories for more effect.

HOW TO MAKE RIBBON BOWS

SINGLE BOW

1. Cross ribbon, forming a loop.

2. Pass the long end away from you.

1. Hold ribbon as shown.

2. Roll around left fingers 7-8 times.

3. Pass round and pull towards you.

5. This way the right side of ribbon always show.

7. Insert this loop into the small loop made in Step 4.

3. Fold in two, with beginning of ribbon at the center.

4. When pulling, twist at back the ribbon to show the right side.

6. With the long end, make another loop.

8. Pull both loops apart to secure.

4. Trim away all four corners.

POMPON BOW

5. Join all the notches.

6. Tie with a narrow ribbon cut into 1/5" width.

7. Hold ends behind the bow.

9. Twist to let stand.

11. Upper loops are done.

8. Pull out inside loop of upper half.

10. Pull out loops rightward, and then leftward alternately.

12. Repeat with the lower half.

ATTACHING RIBBON BOW: A

1. Trim away excess ribbon.

2. Put double-sided tape on the wrong side of bow.

3. Stick it to an appropriate position on the box.

FIGURE-8 BOW

4. Trim away excess.

1. Cross ends of ribbon, leaving about 4" to the end.

5. Pass wire around the cross.

2. Hold the cross tightly.

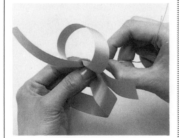

6. Pull wire and secure at back twisting 2-3 times.

3. Make a loop to the other side.

7. Trim away excess wire.

DOUBLE·TRIPLE FIGURE 8 BOW

1. Make a single Figure-8 Bow. Make a loop over the bow.

3. Repeat until triple layers of bows are made. (Repeat more times for a fuller look)

2. Make another lower loop in the same way.

4. Secure the cross with wire, twisting 2-3 times at back.

MAJO-MAJO BOW

1. Make a Triple Figure-8 Bow.

4. Place the bow diagonally on the tied box.

1. Pass ribbon around the box.

4. Then tie a bow on top.

2. Make another Figure-8 Bow over it.

5. Secure it by tying a bow.

2. Place your favorite bow on the cross.

5. Check the balance and trim away excess ribbon.

3. Secure the center with a wire: trim away excess wire at back.

6. If using metallic ribbon, curl ends by pulling between the thumb and back of scissors.

3. Secure the bow by tying with the ribbon from the former tie.

6. Neaten the shape of bow.

WAVE BOW

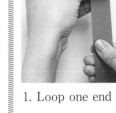

1. Loop one end of ribbon.

1. Hold a ribbon end as shown.

4. Make the same sized loop on the other side.

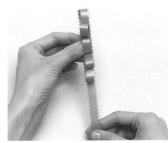

7. Five loops are completed.

2. Twist the longer end under the loop to show the right side.

2. Pass the other end of ribbon around the thumb to make a small loop.

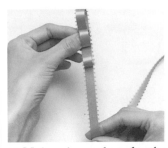

5. Make a larger loop for the bottom layer.

8. Cut off excess end of ribbon near the center on reverse side.

3. Make a little larger loop underneath, to one side.

3. Using the longer end, make a larger loop underneath.

6. Make the same sized loop to the other side.

9. Insert stapler into the center loop and secure.

4. Hold working end towards, the other side.

FRENCH BOW

STAR BOW

4. Repeat until the loops form a star shape.

5. Twist again at center and make a symmetrical loop.

8. Secure the center with wire.

1. With end of ribbon, make a small loop, resembling a cone.

5. Make a small loop in the center.

6. Repeat Step 2-3 to make 4 larger loops, changing direction as shown.

9. Cut off excess wire behind the bow.

2. Make another loop toward you, in the same manner.

6. Cut off excess ribbon.

7. Make a large loop underneath for streamers. Cut off excess.

10. Split the streamer in two.

3. Make a loop at a right angle to previous loops.

7. Staple the center.

CROSS TIE

TRIANGLE TIE

1. With right side of box up, and holding the ribbon at about 12" from the beginning, pass ribbon around the box lengthwise.

4. Pass the short end under the cross.

1. With right side of box up, pass ribbon from center top to bottom at a slant.

4. Let through the wrong side of the box and join the other end at the center.

2. Cross on right side of the box.

5. Pull both ends against each other.

2. Pass around the box to meet the beginning.

5. Cross each other and pass one underneath.

3. Pass around the box, with one end of ribbon.

6. Tie a knot at center.

3. Pass again to the bottom, this time slanting to the other way.

6. Make a single tie at the center top.

WITH RIBBON

DIAGONAL TIE

DOUBLE DIAGONAL TIE

1. With right side of box up, pass ribbon diagonally, leaving about 12" to the end.

4. Bring both ends together.

1. Do as DIAGONAL TIE, Step 1-4. Cross both ends of ribbon at center top.

4. Bring both ends together at the beginning.

2. On wrong side, pull ribbon towards center of a side.

5. Make a single tie at upper right.

2. Pass ribbon diagonally to the other direction, around the box.

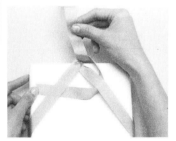

5. Pass one end underneath the last stretch of ribbon.

3. Pass diagonally over right side, parallel to the previous ribbon.

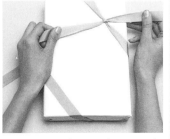

6. Pull ends against each other.

3. Make sure that a diamond is formed on both sides of the box.

6. Make a single tie at the center top.

INSTRUCTIONS

1

MATERIALS:
  Paper: Glossy paper with pattern
  Ribbon: Off white satin ribbon
Other Materials: Sticker
WRAP: Hat Box Wrapping (page 14)
BOW & TIE: Single Tie + Single Bow

MATERIALS:
  Paper: Glossy paper with pattern
  Ribbon: Narrow ribbons, in dark and light brown
Other Materials: Wire
WRAP: Regular Wrapping (page 10)
BOW & TIE: Cross Tie + Double Bow

2

MATERIALS:
  Paper: Glossy paper with pattern
  Ribbon: Dark satin ribbon
Other Materials: Sticker
WRAP: Hat Box Wrapping (page 15)
BOW & TIE: Single Tie + Single Bow

3

MATERIALS:
  Paper: Glossy paper with pattern
  Ribbon: Beige satin ribbon
WRAP: Rolled Wrapping (Rectangle)
BOW & TIE: Arranged Diagonal Tie + Single Bow at center

5

MATERIALS:
  Paper: Glossy paper with pattern
  Ribbon: Narrow ribbons, in dark and light brown
Other Materials: Wire
WRAP: Cylindrical Wrapping (page 15)
BOW & TIE: Cross Tie + 2 Triple Figure-8 Bow layered each other

4

6 · 7
[Pictured on Page 5]
8 - 11
[Pictured on Page 16]

6

MATERIALS:
   Paper: Glossy paper with pattern
   Ribbon: Satin ribbon, Narrow woven gold ribbon
Other Materials: Sticker, Wire
WRAP: Polygonal Wrapping
BOW: Layer 2 Triple Figure-8
Bow TIE: Pass over corners by arranged Cross Tie.

7

MATERIALS:
   Paper: Glossy paper with pattern
   Ribbon: Satin ribbons, in light shades
Other Materials: Sticker, Wire
WRAP: Equilateral Triangle Wrapping
BOW & TIE: Single Tie + Majo-Majo Bow

10

MATERIALS:
   Paper: Wrinkled metallic paper
   Ribbon: Wrinkled metallic ribbons, Metallic curling ribbons, in graded shades
WRAP: Ball Wrapping (page 22)
BOW & TIE: Make sevenfold Figure-8 Bow and attach on top with double-sided tape.

9

MATERIALS:
   Paper: Wrinkled metallic paper
   Ribbon: Wrinkled metallic ribbon, Metallic curling ribbon
Other Materials: Wire
WRAP: Candy Wrapping (page 19)
BOW: Double Figure-8 Bow (page 62)
TIE: Bind the ends with Reflex and attach bow.

8

MATERIALS:
   Paper: Wrinkled metallic paper
   Ribbon: Wrinkled metallic ribbon, Metallic curling ribbon
Other Materials: Sticker, Wire
WRAP: Wrap as for Umbrella Wrapping (page 23) and twist paper all through.
BOW: Triple Bow for the handle edge, Double Bow for the tip
TIE: Wrap around ends with Reflex and tie a knot.

11

MATERIALS:
   Paper: Wrinkled metallic ribbon
   Ribbon: Wrinkled metallic ribbons, Metallic curling ribbon, in varied shades
Other Materials: Wire
WRAP: Wrap as for Teddy Wrapping (page 23)
TIE & BOW: Bind the opening with ribbon, and attach Triple Figure-8 Bow.

MATERIALS:
Paper: Metallic paper
Ribbon: Gold mesh ribbon
Other Materials: Wire
WRAP: Using the technique of Pleated Wrapping (page 26), fold 5 tucks at 1.5cm intervals.
TIE & BOW: Diagonal Tie + Double Figure-8 Bow

16

12 - 15 [Pictured on Page 17]
16 [Pictured on Page 24]

MATERIALS:
Paper: Glossy paper
Ribbon: Wrinkled metallic ribbons, in varied colors
Other Materials: Wire
WRAP: Gather paper toward the center of frypan, as for Ball Wrapping (page 22).
TIE & BOW: Make fifteen-fold Pompon Bow and attach with double-sided tape.

13

14

MATERIALS:
Paper: Clear cellophane with floral pattern
Ribbon: Metallic curling ribbon
WRAP: Teddy Wrapping (page 23).
TIE & BOW: Bind the opening with ribbon, and tie a bow.

15

MATERIALS:
Paper: Wrinkled metallic paper
Ribbons: Wrinkled metallic ribbons, Metallic curling ribbon, in varied shades paper
Other Materials: Sticker, Wire
WRAP: Make tucks around the neck of bottle as for Wrapping Plump Bottle (page 18).
BOW: Double Figure-8 Bow (page 62)
TIE: Wrap around the neck of bottle with Reflex, and attach bow by tying another bow.

12

MATERIALS:
Paper: Clear cellophane with floral pattern
Ribbon: Wrinkled metallic ribbon
Other Materials: Wire
WRAP: Make pleats toward the top as for Melon Wrapping (page 22).
TIE & BOW: Make Double French Bow and attach to the top with double-sided tape.

MATERIALS:
  Paper: Glossy paper with pattern
  Ribbon: Silver mesh ribbon
WRAP: Triangular Fold (page 33)
TIE & BOW: Pass ribbon across corners, using the method for Diagonal Tie: tie a bow

MATERIALS:
  Paper: Glossy paper with pattern
  Ribbon: Metallic mesh ribbon in matching color
Other Materials: Wire
WRAP: Regular Wrapping. Cut different paper into strips of the box width and fold corners to form triangles; wrap the box with it and secure with double-sided tape.

MATERIALS:
  Paper: Glossy paper
  Ribbon: Metallic mesh ribbon in contrasting color
WRAP: Rectangular Fold (page 32)
TIE & BOW: Single Tie + Single Bow

MATERIALS:
  Paper: Glossy paper, in solid color and pattern
  Ribbon: Metallic mesh ribbon in matching color
WRAP: Using the method for Wrapping with Insertion (paper doiley, see page 29) fan out strips of paper; staple and insert under the flap.
TIE & BOW: Single Tie + Single Bow

MATERIALS:
  Paper: Glossy paper
  Ribbon: Silver mesh ribbon
WRAP: Diagonal Wrapping. Top with accordion-fold and secure with double-sided tape.

MATERIALS:
  Paper: Glossy paper with pattern
WRAP: Diagonal Wrapping (page 7)
TIE & BOW: Using the same paper, make a bow shape and attach with double-sided tape.

71

23 - 28
[Pictured on Page
38-39]

MATERIALS:
Paper: Glossy paper with
pattern
Ribbons: Satin ribbons, in
varied widths and colors
WRAP: Make Shirt-Collar
Bag (page 44).
TIE & BOW: Wrap around the
neck with ribbon and tie a
bow.

23

MATERIALS:
Ribbon: Satin ribbons, in
varied widths and colors
Other Materials: Wire
BOW: Fourteen-fold Figure-8
Bow
TIE: Arranged Cross Tie

25

24

28

MATERIALS:
Paper: Air bubble bag
Ribbon: Metallic curling
ribbon
TIE & BOW: Tie in Cross Tie
twice, tie a knot and curl
ends.

MATERIALS:
Paper: Glossy paper with
pattern
Ribbon: Satin ribbon in
contrasting color
BOX: Variation of Decorating
Box: B (page 42)
TIE & BOW: 2 rounds of
Single Tie and tie a bow.

26

MATERIALS:
Wrapper: Clear cellophane
with floral pattern
Ribbon: Yellow satin ribbon
Other Materials: Wire
WRAP: Put gift in the bag,
and bind the opening.
BOW: Fourfold Figure-8
Bow
TIE: Bind the opening with
ribbon, and attach bow.

MATERIALS:
Paper: Clear cellophane
with floral pattern
Ribbon: Red satin ribbon
WRAP: Put gift in the bag,
and bind the opening.
TIE & BOW: Bind the opening
with ribbon, and tie a bow.

27

MATERIALS:
   Paper: *Unryu washi*, Wrinkled *washi*
Ribbon: Satin ribbon with gold flecks
Other Materials: Wire
WRAP: Wrap box as for Regular wrapping. Fold another paper on the bias to the box width, and wring.
TIE & BOE: Make Triple Figure-8 Bow with Magical Tube. Wrap around the joint of paper with ribbon, place Figure-8 Bow and tie a bow to hold it.

29　[Pictured on Page 39]
79 - 82　[Pictured on Page 58]

MATERIALS:
   Paper: Patterned *washi*, Wrinkled *washi* Ribbon: Satin ribbon in matching color
Other Materials: Mizuhiki, Wire
WRAP: Wrap the box with wrinkled *washi* (Regular Wrapping). Fold patterned *Washi* into the box width; wrap around box and join at top.
TIE & BOW: Using wire, form Mizuhiki into figure-8 plus a circle. Wrap around the top of box with ribbon and tie. Pull out ribbons through Mizuhiki circle, and tie a bow.

MATERIALS:
   Paper: *Unryu washi*, Patterned *washi*
WRAP: Join both sheets of paper with glue. Overlap both edges, press down and tape. Lift up far and near papers and overlap at center. Lift up sides and tie a knot.

MATERIALS:
   Paper: *Unryu washi*, in varied shades
Ribbon: Matte ribbon in subdued color, Tube ribbon
Other Materials: Wire
WRAP: Wrap box in Regular Wrapping. Fold another paper into a triangle, sliding the apex. Gather paper at the top of box; secure with wire. Wrap around the bind to conceal the wire, and tie a bow.

MATERIALS:
   Paper: Paper bag with handles
   Ribbon: Matte ribbon in subdued color, Tube ribbon
TIE & BOW: Remove handles, and thread ribbon through the holes; tie a bow.

INSTRUCTIONS

Brief instructions for page 50

32 MATERIALS:
   Paper: Floral pattern paper
   Ribbon: Woven white ribbon
   with gold trim
   WRAPPING: Diagonal wrapping
   (page 7)
   TYING: Cross tie (page 66)
   Recular bow (page 60)

33 MATERIALS:
   Paper: Solid color paper
   Ribbon: Sheer ribbon
   WRAPPING: Diagonal wrapping
   (page 7)
   TYING: Cross tie (page 66)
   Majo-Majo bow (page 63)

34 MATERIALS:
   Paper: Floral pattern paper
   Ribbon: Satin ribbon in matching color
   WRAPPING: Regular wrapping
   (page 10)
   TYING: Cross tie (page 66)
   Double bow

30 MATERIALS:
   Bag: Flat paper bag
   Ribbon: Sheer ribbon in matching color
   WRAPPING:
   TYING: Make a triple figure-8
   Majo-Majo bow (page 63).
   Bind the opening and secure
   with ribbon.

31 MATERIALS:
   Paper: Floral pattern paper
   Ribbon: Sheer ribbon in matching color
   WRAPPING: Cylinder Wrapping
   (page 15)
   TYING: Variation of Cross tie
   (page 66) with Regular Bow
   (page 60)

37 MATERIALS:
    Paper: Mat paper in subdued
    color
    Ribbon: Satin ribbons, in
    varied colors
    WRAPPING: Rolled Wrapping
    (page 9)
    TYING: Variation of Triangle tie
    (page 66) with Majo-Majo bow
    (page 63)

38 MATERIALS:
    Paper: *Unryu-washi*, with gold
    flecks
    Ribbon: Satin ribbons, in
    varied colors
    WRAPPING: Wrapping Polygon
    (page 11)
    TYING: Variation of Cross tie
    (page 66) each side Majo-
    Majo bow (page 63)

39 MATERIALS:
    Bag: Satin fabric gift bag
    Ribbon: Sheer striped ribbon,
    Narrow satin ribbon, in match-
    ing shades
    WRAPPING: Soft Toy Wrapping
    (page 23)
    TYING: Bind the opening and
    secure with ribbon

35 MATERIALS:
    Paper: Mat solid color paper
    Ribbon: Satin ribbons
    WRAPPING: Bottle wrapping
    (page 18)
    TYING: Secure Majo-Majo bow
    (page 63)

36 MATERIALS:
    Paper: *Unryu-washi*
    Ribbon: Satin ribbons, in pas-
    tel shades
    WRAPPING: Diagonal wrapping
    (page 18)
    TYING: Cross tie (page 66)
    Majo-Majo bow (page 63)

42 MATERIALS:
Paper: Glossy white paper
Ribbon: Sheer white ribbon
with gold trim
WRAPPING: Diagonal wrapping
(page 7)
TYING: Cross tie (page 66) with
Regular bow (page 60)

43 MATERIALS:
Paper: Glossy white paper
Ribbon: Gold mesh ribbon
Narrow metallic curling ribbon
WRAPPING: Wrapping Hexagon
(page 11)
TYING: Variation of Cross tie
(page 66) for each side.
Double Majo-Majo bow (page
63)

44 MATERIALS:
Paper: Floral pattern paper
Ribbon: Tulle lace ribbon
Metallic curling ribbon
WRAPPING: Wrapping round box
(page 14)
TYING: Single tie
Double Majo-Majo bow (page
63)

45 MATERIALS:
Paper: Glossy white paper
Ribbon: Narrow sheer ribbon
with gold trim
TYING: Cross tie (page 66)
Majo-Majo bow (page 63)

40 MATERIALS:
Paper: Floral pattern paper
Ribbon: Woven white ribbon
WRAPPING: Regular Wrapping
(page 10)
TYING: Cross tie (page 66)
Double bow

41 MATERIALS:
Paper: Clear cellophane with
floral pattern
Ribbon: Woven white ribbon
WRAPPING: Place the cellophane over the Regular wrapping (page 10), then wrap again
in Ball wrapping method.
TYING: Gather the top and
secure the bow.

46 MATERIALS:
Paper: Wrinkled *washi*
WRAPPING: Regular Wrapping
(page 10)

48 MATERIALS:
Bag: Satin fabric gift bag
Ribbon: Sheer stripe ribbon,
Narrow satin ribbon
Other: materials: Silk rosebuds
WRAPPING: Soft Toy wrapping
(page 23)
TYING: Bind the opening and
secure with ribbon

50 MATERIALS:
Paper: *Unryu-washi*
Ribbon: Sheer striped ribbon
with picot edging
WRAPPING: Diagonal wrapping
(page 7)
TYING: Cross tie (page 66)
Regular bow (page 60)

47 MATERIALS:
Paper: *Unryu-washi*
Ribbon: Mother's Day ribbon
with lace edging
WRAPPING: Diagonal Wrapping
(page 7)
TYING: Triangle tie (page 66)
Majo-Majo bow (page 63)

49 MATERIALS:
Paper: Patterned *washi*
Ribbon: Satin ribbon with stich
pattern
WRAPPING: Bouquet Wrapping
(page 21)
TYING: Gather the bottom and
secure the French bow (page
65)

Brief instructions for page 53

BOW KNOT

Completed bow knot.

This knot unties if streamers are pulled.

1. Using long enough ribbon for streamers, cross left end over the right.

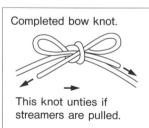

2. Pass the front end under, and tie.

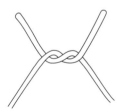

3. Fold both ends.

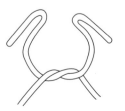

4. Cross the folds in right over left fashion, and tie.

5. Pull the folds to tighten the knot.

WARNING!

If the folds are crossed in left over right fashion, they form so-called '*Tatemusubi*', which looks untidy.

55 MATERIALS:
Paper: Tartan plaid paper
WRAPPING: Regular Wrapping
(page 10)

56 MATERIALS:
Paper: Glossy white paper
Ribbon: Satin ribbon with lace
edging
WRAPPING: Regular Wrapping
(page 10)
TYING: Cross tie (page 66) with
Majo-Majo bow (page 63)

57 MATERIALS:
Paper: Glossy lime-color paper
WRAPPING: Wrapping Round
Box (page 14)

58 MATERIALS:
Paper: Glossy paper
Ribbon: Satin ribbon with stich
pattern, in matching color
WRAPPING: Wrapping Round
Box (page 14)
TYING: French bow (page 65)

59 MATERIALS:
Paper: Glossy lime-color paper
Ribbon: Satin ribbon with stich
pattern, in matching color
WRAPPING: Triangle Wrapping
(page 12)
TYING: French bow (page 65)

60 MATERIALS:
Wrapper: Patterned box
Ribbon: Message ribbon in
matching color
WRAPPING: Commercial gift box
TYING: Cross Tie (page 66)
Regular Bow (page 60)

61 MATERIALS:
Wrapper: Gold hat box
Paper: Narrow satin ribbon
with picot edging
Ribbon: Feather Edge
WRAPPING: Paste the Metallic
Satin over the cylinder shape
box.
TYING: Variation of Cross tie
(page 66)
Majo-Majo bow (page 63)

Brief instructions for page 55

66 MATERIALS:
  Paper: White paper with pattern
  Ribbon: Black tulle lace ribbon
WRAPPING: Hexagon Wrapping (page 11)
TYING: Cross Tie (page 66) with Majo-Majo bow (page 63)

67 MATERIALS:
  Paper: Patterned black paper
WRAPPING: Regular Wrapping (page 10)

68 MATERIALS:
  Paper: Patterned paper
  Ribbon: Matte red ribbon
WRAPPING: Regular Wrapping (page 10)
TYING: Cross Tie (page 66) with Regular bow (page 63)

69 MATERIALS:
  Paper: Glossy black paper
  Ribbon: Black satin ribbon, Narrow gold ribbon
  Other materials: Silk rosebud
WRAPPING: Commercial Gift Box
TYING: Double bow. secure the rose bud with Glue Gun in the center, then bind with double-sided tape.

62 MATERIALS:
  Paper: Patterned paper
WRAPPING: Cylinder wrapping (page 15)

63 MATERIALS: Monotone gingham pattern paper
WRAPPING: Triangle wrapping (page 12)

64 MATERIALS:
  Paper: Glossy black paper
  Ribbon: Black satin ribbon, Narrow gold ribbon
WRAPPING: Triangle Wrapping (page 12)
TYING: Single Tie
  Majo-Majo bow (page 63)

65 MATERIALS:
  Paper: Glossy black paper
  Ribbon: White red ribbon, in matte finish
WRAPPING: Diagonal Wrapping (page 7)
TYING: Cross Tie (page 66) with Regular bow (page 60)

Brief instructions for page 56-57

74 MATERIALS:
Paper: Glossy green paper
Ribbon: Red/green pattern ribbon
WRAPPING: Wrapping hexagon (page 11)
TYING: Variation Cross tie (page 66)
Majo-Majo bow (page 63)

75 MATERIALS:
Paper: Christmas gift bag
Ribbon: Green satin ribbon
WRAPPING: Use commercial gift bag
TYING: Gather the bag with wire and secure a French bow. (page 65)

76 MATERIALS:
Paper: Glossy green paper
Ribbon: Green/gold striped ribbon, Narrow gold ribbon
WRAPPING: Round box wrapping (page 14)
TYING: Make Double bow with New Cotton Christmas, secure the Majo-Majo bow (page 63) of 2 French Metallic color.

70 MATERIALS:
Paper: Glossy green paper
Ribbon: Satin ribbon in matching shade
WRAPPING: Triangle wrapping (page 12)
TYING: Variation of Diagonal tie (page 67) with Majo-Majo bow (page 63)

71 MATERIALS:
Paper: Glossy green paper
Ribbon: Red satin ribbon, red/green striped ribbon
WRAPPING: Cylinder Wrapping (page 14)
TYING: Variation of Cross tie (page 66) with red ribbon. Make Double bow with Cotton Christmas, gather with wire, then secure with red ribbon. (page 60)

72 MATERIALS:
Paper: Glossy green paper
Ribbon: Wide ribbon in red/green pattern
WRAPPING: Cylinder Wrapping (page 15)
TYING: Bind the ribbon around the cylinder and secure with double-sided tape.

73 MATERIALS:
Paper: Glossy paper
Accessories: Green tinsel, Birds, Pine cones, mitsumata
WRAPPING: Regular Wrapping
TYING: Cross tie (page 66) Majo-Majo Bow(Page63) Secure the Majo-Majo bow and put the Mitsumata, pine cones on it with glue gun.

77 MATERIALS:
Paper: Glossy green paper
Other materials: Greeting card with Christmas ornament
WRAPPING: Regular wrapping (page 10)
TYING: Secure the ornament with card.

78 MATERIALS:
Paper: Glossy green paper
Ribbon: Green ribbons, in solid color and pattern
Other materials: Greeting card with christmas ornament
WRAPPING: Regular wrapping
TYING: Single tie with Regal Satin.
Double bow New Cotton Christmas
Put the Regular bow (page 60) with Regal Satin on top.

INDEX